SO-AZQ-804

Pebble™

Desert Animals

Ostriches

by William John Ripple

Consulting Editor: Gail Saunders-Smith, PhD

Capstone *press*

Mankato, Minnesota

Pebble Books are published by Capstone Press,
151 Good Counsel Drive, P.O. Box 669, Mankato, Minnesota 56002.
www.capstonepress.com

1 2 3 4 5 6 10 09 08 07 06 05

Library of Congress Cataloging-in-Publication Data
Ripple, William John.
  Ostriches / by William John Ripple.
    p. cm.—(Desert animals)
  Includes bibliographical references and index.
  ISBN 0-7368-3636-5 (hardcover)
    1. Ostriches—Juvenile literature. I. Title. II. Desert animals (Mankato, Minn.)
QL696.S9R57 2005
598.5′24—dc22   2004013300

Summary: Simple text and photographs introduce the habitat, appearance, and
behavior of ostriches.

Note to Parents and Teachers

The Desert Animals set supports national science standards related
to life science. This book describes and illustrates ostriches. The
photographs support early readers in understanding the text. The
repetition of words and phrases helps early readers learn new
words. This book also introduces early readers to subject-specific
vocabulary words, which are defined in the Glossary section. Early
readers may need assistance to read some words and to use the
Table of Contents, Glossary, Read More, Internet Sites, and Index
sections of the book.

Table of Contents

4

What Are Ostriches?

Ostriches are
the biggest birds
in the world.

Male ostriches have
black and white feathers.
Female ostriches have
brown and gray feathers.

places where wild ostriches live

Where Ostriches Live

Wild ostriches live in deserts and grasslands in Africa. Deserts are dry areas with few plants.

Body Parts

Ostriches have
long necks
and long legs.
Ostriches run fast.

Ostriches have
short wings.
Ostriches are
too heavy to fly.

Ostriches have big eyes and long eyelashes.

What Ostriches Do

Ostriches live in groups called flocks.

Ostriches eat grass, leaves, and insects.

Female ostriches lay eggs.
They sit on their eggs
during the day.
Male ostriches sit on
the eggs at night.

Glossary

desert—an area of dry land with few plants; deserts receive very little rain.

eyelashes—stiff feathers on the edge of an ostrich's eyelid; eyelashes help keep sand and dirt out of an ostrich's eyes.

feather—one of the light, fluffy parts that covers a bird's body; feathers protect an ostrich's skin; feathers keep ostriches warm during cool desert nights.

grasslands—open land covered mostly by grass; grasslands have few trees.

Read More

Green, Jen. *Ostriches.* Animal Families. Danbury, Conn.: Grolier Educational, 2001.

Jacobs, Liza. *Ostriches.* Wild Wild World. San Diego: Blackbirch Press, 2004.

Whitehouse, Patricia. *Ostrich.* Zoo Animals. Chicago: Heinemann Library, 2003.

Internet Sites

FactHound offers a safe, fun way to find Internet sites related to this book. All of the sites on FactHound have been researched by our staff.

Here's how:

1. Visit *www.facthound.com*

2. Type in this special code **0736836365** for age-appropriate sites. Or enter a search word related to this book for a more general search.

3. Click on the **Fetch It** button.

FactHound will fetch the best sites for you!

Index

Word Count: 97
Grade: 1
Early-Intervention Level: 11

Editorial Credits

Mari C. Schuh, editor; Patrick D. Dentinger, set designer and illustrator; Steve Meunier, photo researcher; Scott Thoms, photo editor

Photo Credits

Ann and Rob Simpson, 12
Bruce Coleman Inc./Clem Haagner, 20; Danilo Donadoni, 8; J & D Bartlett, 10; John Shaw, 6
Corbis/Carl & Ann Purcell, 18
Digital Vision, 14
Manaan Kar Ray, 1
Robin Brandt, cover, 4, 16